harbngers

harb ngers

essays

B.J. HOLLARS

BULL★CITY
PRESS

DURHAM, NORTH CAROLINA

Harbingers

Published in the United States of America

"Harbingers" was previously published
in the *Cincinnati Review.*
"The Loneliness of Oppenheimer" was previously published
in *Boulevard.*
"Fragments for Medgar" was previously published
in *American Literary Review.*

Library of Congress Cataloging-in-Publication Data

Hollars, B.J.
Harbingers: essays / by B.J. Hollars
p. cm.
ISBN-13: 978-1-949344-07-3

Book design by Spock and Associates
Cover photo by Osman Rana
Author photo by Justin Patchin

Published by
BULL CITY PRESS
1217 Odyssey Drive
Durham, NC 27713

www.BullCityPress.com

CONTENTS

For my students—
may you make the future better than the past.

And for Eric Rasmussen and Brendan Todt—
so clear-eyed and committed.

HARBINGERS

My mother calls on a Saturday morning in September.

"There's something I need to tell you," she says.

"Okay," I say, adjusting the phone while keeping one hand on the wheel. "What is it?"

I'm en route from my home in Eau Claire, Wisconsin, nearly finished with a two-hundred-mile drive to the eastern side of the state.

A moment of static, of cross-connection.

"You know, let me call you right back. I'm about to check out at the grocery."

"Sure, but . . ."

Click.

It's not like my mother to hold back, not like her to hang up on me, either. For the five interminable minutes that follow, I diagnose her with every crippling ailment I know. Once I've settled upon any number of dire scenarios (cancer, Alzheimer's, etc.), my mind leaps to a simpler darkness: a future document on my desktop saved as Mom_Obit.doc.

I'm shaken from my stupor by the buzz of my phone.

This is how it begins, I think.

"What is it?" I say.

"Well," she says, "it's like my grandmother used to say: Everything's fine now."

She tells me about her EKG and her echo, how the doctors

heard her heart and what it said.

"Everything's fine *now*," she repeats. "It's just that some of my blood is running backward."

"Blood can do that?"

"It's called moderate tricuspid valve regurgitation," she recites, which to my ear sounds like a dental problem, a car problem, and a digestive problem all rolled into one. "But don't worry," she's quick to add. "It can be managed with diet and exercise."

"So you're . . . relatively okay?"

"Oh, sure," she says. "I mostly just called to make sure you are. To encourage you to see a doctor."

"Because my blood might be running backward, too?"

"No," she says. "But our family has a history of high blood pressure and heart problems and—"

"—blood running backward?"

She laughs. "Look, Beegee, all I'm saying is you're no spring chicken anymore. You never know what's going on inside of you."

Which, at thirty-one, is exactly how I like it. Nevertheless, since she's my mother and her heart is burdened enough, I agree to make an appointment.

"Thank you," she says. "That's all I ask."

I've barely hung up when, to my left, I see a pair of suit-coated men wheeling a light-blue coffin into a church.

*

Two months before my mother's call, on a warm night in July, my family and I are swarmed by mayflies, caught up in their cloud of abdomens, thoraxes, and heads. My father, brother, wife, three-year-old son, and I observe the onslaught while clutching ice cream cones on the north shore of the Wisconsin River. We're on vacation, and since we don't know what to do with our nights, we've ended up here—not for the flies but for the ferry, whose passage makes for good evening entertainment.

We watch as a brigade of thousands engages in frenetic flight. It's as if they cannot live fast enough. They have survived two molts and, upon shedding their exteriors for the last time, are left with wings thinner than cheesecloth and twice as fragile.

My brother snaps a photo as their frenzy winds down, as they begin to drift to the street signs and the fence posts that surround us. They clutter every inch of landing strip they've got, settling in for their first and last night above the waterline.

My son—his face smeared with blueberry ice cream—tugs my pant leg and asks if we can go back to the rental house in nearby Merrimac to see Grandma and his baby sister.

"Finish your cone first," I say, entranced by the shimmer of wings in the waning light.

*

Later, days before my mother's call, I'm stirred from my morning reading by my dog scratching at my jeans. I reach for the leash, for my son's hand, and we begin our stroll around the block. As usual, my thirteen-pound mixed breed pulls with the gusto of a seasoned sled dog, releasing a wheezing noise that's embarrassing for us both. She's convinced herself there's some new smell right around the corner, despite my assurances that there's nothing new. Not in this neighborhood, at least, where we put a premium on constancy. The smells don't change and our neighbors don't change and neither do our routines.

After three years of these walks, we have become a fixture in the routine. Twice daily, the neighbors expect to see the wheezing animal and her sidekicks, and twice daily we don't disappoint. In return, we expect the same constancy of their own quotidian behaviors—porch sitting, weed pulling, sweeping out the garage. With each lap around the block, we do our best to fulfill our Midwestern obligation to friendliness and congeniality, offering a smile, a wave, and the right amount of reassuring small talk.

But on this particular morning there's a disruption. Something is not okay in the home belonging to our elderly neighbors. I don't know their names, but on countless mornings and nights my son and I have gabbed with the old man as he adjusted the sprinkler on his lawn.

On this morning, however, we watch as a young woman I've never seen drives him away from his home.

During the afternoon walk, my dog and I witness their return. The man is wearing a suit coat and clutching flowers, eyes down as he trails the young woman back to his front door.

My dog pulls, catching his eye, and he notices me noticing him.

He offers no smile, no wave.

His eyes tell me his wife is dead.

*

An hour has passed since my mother's phone call, and though I'm still rattled by the news, my worry has begun to subside. Or at least change forms. Now I'm worrying about me, and I turn down the audiobook—Edward Abbey's *Desert Solitaire*—and listen for the sound of my blood.

I stop listening when I reach my destination: Horicon, Wisconsin. I'm here because Brady, my nature-loving former student, has promised me a canoe, a paddle, and all the wilderness I can handle. Since I want to be the guy who wants wilderness—the professor for whom nature is more than a theme in nineteenth-century literature—I agreed.

Brady and I arrive at the boat landing midmorning and, after negotiating the canoe from the hood of the car to the water's edge, begin our two-man bobble into the seats. We don't tip—a small victory—and as the canoe steadies beneath us, I take a moment to settle my nerves.

We try to paddle beyond the cattails, but there's no paddling beyond cattails—not here, at least, where they grow as thick as a wall. Since we can't see over them, we never quite know what's ahead—a predicament that helps me better understand why my dog pulls so hard on her leash. Like her, I'm excited by the prospect of some new something right around the corner, which for us includes an egret, a heron, and an upland sandpiper.

At least we think it's an upland sandpiper. We refer to our field guides, the two of us flipping pages as fast as we can to identify the bird before it leaves us.

Brady, always the good student, finds it first.

"Yup, upland sandpiper," he says as we bob in that stillness. "It's gotta be."

"Gotta be," I repeat, grateful for his certainty.

*

Mayflies are born mouthless, the mouth unnecessary given the brevity of their lives. Their work is simply to reproduce, a task they perform with orgiastic zeal.

Our family sees a bit of their courtship on the shores of the Wisconsin River, but mostly all we see are mayflies wrapping it up. Their wings grow heavy with the first whisper of death, their fuel gauges rattling toward empty. Is there any better reminder of *carpe diem* than observing a lifecycle that allows for only a single day?

During our week at the rental house, we take a cue from those mayflies. We turn off the TV and wage war with water balloons. We leave our phones inside and take to the paths in the woods. One morning, we observe a bumblebee hovering near the top of a flower head; one evening, we spot a pair of sandhill cranes in a field.

*

My son and I continue our dog-walk routine, but my elderly neighbor is rarely out anymore; summer is gone, and he has no need for a sprinkler. Still, his grass grows, and as we pass his house, we spot the young woman raking the clippings from his yard. She sees us, and I smile and wave. She returns both in kind, adopting the script her father and I have already written.

I'm content with our interaction, proof that everything in our lives is okay. But everything isn't—not for her—and though I know it's a risk, one evening I breach protocol.

"I've noticed there've been a lot of cars here these past few days," I say.

I don't know what response I expect, and her silence confirms that she doesn't know either.

"What I mean," I retry, "is if something has happened, and if there's something we can do to help, we'd be glad to. We live just a few houses down."

The woman stares at us, a faraway smile glossing her face. The tines bend as she leans against her rake, and then, after a moment's hesitation, she thanks me. She tells me her mother has just died.

"I'm sorry," I say. "If there's anything we can do . . ."

The dog pulls, so I wave goodbye, leaving her to the grass clippings.

A moment later we turn the corner, and there is, at last, a new smell. Standing before us in the gloaming is a pair of whitetail deer.

For the first time in her life, the dog does not pull. She sits, letting the leash hang loose.

*

From the canoe, the only animals we see are birds: gulls,

cormorants, and eight pelicans piercing the sky. Each sighting is thrilling in its own way, yet what thrills me most has nothing to do with birds.

It's the unexpected thrumming coming from beneath the hull.

Thud-thud-thud-thud-thud!

"Jesus!" I shout as the boat rocks, sending the water rippling. "What the hell is that?"

We sit in silence, waiting for whatever is beneath to pass.

Then, a moment later: *thud-thud-thud-thud-thud!*

"Are those otters?" I shout, peering over the edge of the canoe. "Are there otters here?"

"Maybe," Brady says, grabbing the gunwale. "Could be, I guess."

The birds scatter overhead, their silhouettes fast approaching the limits of binocular range.

Our muscles tense as we grip our paddles. We wait for whatever comes next.

*

During a family walk on our last night of vacation in Merrimac, we cross paths with the only other renters on the property—a married couple with a pair of kids who are staying in the place up the hill.

After a few minutes of chitchat, the father leans in.

"Listen," he says, "you all didn't hear anything strange last night, did you?"

It's an odd question, made odder still by the glance he gives his wife.

"No . . . I don't think so," my mother says, turning to my father. "Did you?"

My father shrugs.

"So you didn't hear the wolves, then?"

Our eyes widen.

"Sometime after midnight," the man continues. "They were really going at it. From somewhere over that way."

He points to the tall grass on the far side of the property. His wife nods.

"Anyway, just keep your guard up," he says. "You wouldn't want to spook 'em."

*

In the predawn dark before setting out for the canoe trip—before hearing about my mother's heart—I walked the dog under the streetlights. Just as we approached the home of my newly widowed neighbor, I spotted a pair of shadows in the grass.

The deer were back, doe and fawn. Again, my dog sat still.

We watched them watch us. At last, there was no static, no cross-connection. I divined a destiny where that elderly man would one day return to his sprinkler. I blinked. The deer began their retreat back into the woods, leaving my dog and me to sort through what remained: a scent, a memory, a hoof print pressed into the earth.

That night I wrote a letter to my neighbor, sharing with him the good news.

Not to worry, it read, *because there were deer in your lawn this morning.*

I considered telling him about my mother, and the mayflies, and the sandpiper—all the things I knew for sure. And telling him, too, of the things that remained less certain: the otters and the wolves.

All of it means something, I wrote. *We just don't always know what.*

Then I tossed my note into the bin.

The world is noisy enough without me.

THE LONELINESS OF OPPENHEIMER

✳ **1** ✳

In the beginning, God created heaven and earth. Then, we
saw fit to destroy them. The first blast, known as the Trinity
Test, occurred in New Mexico's Jornada del Muerto desert, an
uninhabited shrub-brush landscape stretching 100 miles north
to south. A breathtakingly empty place. The kind of place,
scientists believed, that could withstand an atomic test without
much notice. At 5:29 a.m. on July 16, 1945, those scientists
were proven wrong. There was no way to conduct an atomic
test discreetly. Two hundred and eighty miles to the west, the
citizens of Amarillo rubbed their eyes and marveled at the
changed horizon.

❋ 2 ❋

Perched on Campania Hill just 20 miles out, *New York Times* reporter William Laurence observed the blast. "And just at that instant there rose as if from the bowels of the earth a light not of this world, the light of many suns in one. It was a sunrise such as the world had never seen," he wrote, "a great green supersun climbing in a fraction of a second to a height of more than eight thousand feet, rising ever higher until it touched the clouds, lighting up earth and sky all around with a dazzling luminosity."

✳ **3** ✳

In the moments prior to denotation, 425 scientists, engineers, and military personnel anxiously awaited to be dazzled. Some were stationed in outposts, others trenches, and all wore welding goggles. Despite their calculations, none of them knew for certain what the bomb's effects would be on themselves or their landscape. And so, the betting began. Who among them could most accurately guess, to the nearest kiloton, the amount of energy unleashed upon the world that day? Who among them could guess destruction best?

❄ 4 ❄

Physicist Isidor Rabi, the man lucky enough to take home the $102 pot, appeared to have guessed best. In truth, the Columbia professor was simply the last to enter the pool. He'd settled with the only option that remained: 18 kilotons—just a smidge shy of the 18.6 kilotons of TNT they'd detonated.

✳ 5 ✳

Deep in the desert that day, men and women celebrated their success. They believed they'd seen what humans had never seen before: a glimpse of the end of the world. Rabi passed around a bottle of whiskey while others formed a conga line. Though it wasn't yet 6:00 a.m., 41-year-old J. Robert Oppenheimer—the bomb's father—shared a brandy with his brother, Frank. When that failed to calm Oppenheimer's nerves, Rabi drove him away from the site and into the quiet New Mexican hills. "Behind them," one reporter wrote, "the fallout cloud drifted in the distance."

✳ **6** ✳

Seventy-two years later, my wife and I touch down in
Albuquerque, just a few hours north of the blast site. Neither
of us knows quite why we're here. All we know is that we want
to get away from the world for a while. To wave goodbye to our
four-year-old and our two-year-old and vanish for a couple
of days. Detach. Unplug. Disconnect. Leave the worrying to
somebody else. Back home we'd been contending with subzero
weather, and we assumed New Mexico could offer something
warmer. It did—30 degrees. That night, after driving our rental
car to Santa Fe, we toast our trip over margaritas in the empty
hotel bar. "To 30 degrees," I say, and I mean it. *To being alone,* I
think, and I mean that, too.

※ **7** ※

There's a difference between being lonely and being alone—the latter is a state, and the former, a condition of that state. When experienced in the proper proportions, being alone can feel quite good. Yet in the improper proportions, being alone can be a killer. Studies have shown that poor social relationships are associated with increased risk for coronary heart disease. Which is not to be confused with a broken heart.

✳ **8** ✳

Ella Oppenheimer—the mother of the father of the bomb—died in 1931 of leukemia, 14 years prior to her son's achievement. That October, 27-year-old Robert, a professor at Berkeley, had traveled from California to New York to cherish what little time they had left together. Soon after her death, he was visited by a former teacher, Herbert Smith, who comforted his pupil as best he could. But the fissure could not be fixed. With eyes as blue as mountain flowers, Oppenheimer turned to Smith and whispered, "I'm the loneliest man in the world."

☀ **9** ☀

By 1936, he began to feel a little less lonely—the result of falling
in love with a graduate student named Jean Tatlock. In their
early years, everyone who saw them bore witness to their love.
A mutual friend remarked that other women were jealous of
Oppenheimer's affections toward Tatlock. "His precocity and
brilliance already legend, he walked his jerky walk, feet turned
out, a Jewish Pan with his blue eyes and his wild Einstein hair."
He was handsome, brilliant, and as he beelined round the quad,
unmistakable.

✳ **10** ✳

On our last day in Santa Fe, I stumble upon an antique store far off the main drag. It's a warehouse next to a cemetery next to a highway. Inside, I find a treasure trove of trinkets: turquoise, belt buckles, all the usual fare. In a booth near the back, I spot a photograph of 25 men and women seated around a long table. The description on the back reads: "Vintage Photo from Los Alamos—guess who's at Dinner?" The woman working the booth wanders my way. She says she thinks the man at the head of the table is Oppenheimer. I squint, searching his facial features. Indeed, he resembles the pictures I've seen; he possesses the same head shape, the same body type, the same style of handkerchief peeking from his breast pocket. But his eyebrows appear less bushy, and his smile's not quite right. She tells me she snagged it at an estate sale in Los Alamos, that you find all kinds of things out there in the desert. I walk the photo to the cash register, fork over the money, and leave.

❋ **11** ❋

Today, there's no mistaking Oppenheimer or what he represents. Dubbed the "American Prometheus" by his biographers, it's a title he's more than earned. After all, he, like the Titan himself, gave humans an impossible gift. As the Greek poet Hesiod recounts, while visiting Mount Olympus, Prometheus snagged fire in a fennel stalk and offered its flames to humankind. That Titan civilized us; he gave us the warmth and protection we required.

✳ 12 ✳

Following the success of the Trinity Test, Oppenheimer gave us a semblance of warmth and protection, too. Americans loved the bomb—named drinks and desserts in honor of it. We even dressed a showgirl in a mushroom-cloud dress and paid her to dance around. We loved it because it was ours and ours alone—until it wasn't. On August 29, 1949, when the Soviets conducted their own successful nuclear test, our love for the bomb began to lessen. Perhaps it was foolhardy to think that we alone could hold fire in a fennel stalk. But the blast, so beautiful, had blinded us to any other possibility. At 5:29 a.m. on that July morning, all we saw was the future when, in fact, we should have looked to the past, should have remembered how Zeus chained Prometheus to a mountaintop and sent an eagle to eat his liver daily. Night after night, his liver regrew, and day after day, the eagle ate it.

✳ **13** ✳

Surely there is some metaphor to be had here, and surely
we will bend it until it conforms to the story we need. Insert
America in place of the eagle, for instance, and Prometheus in
place of our enemies. But how can this be? Isn't Oppenheimer
our Prometheus? And if so, why would our hero ever be made
to endure such a fate? Had he fallen out of favor with the
gods? Following the bombing of Hiroshima and Nagasaki, a
conflicted Oppenheimer struggled with whether to support the
continued usage of the weapon he'd helped create. Struggled,
too, to support the creation of a greater weapon, the hydrogen
bomb. For some, his attitude—the notion of restraint—seemed
downright un-American. What good was fire in a fennel stalk if
we couldn't wave it around at our enemies?

✳ **14** ✳

On October 16, 1945, General Leslie Groves presented the Los Alamos Laboratory a certificate of appreciation. Upon accepting the honor, Oppenheimer made his antinuclear sentiments clear. "If atomic bombs are to be added to the arsenals of a warring world, or to the arsenals of nations preparing for war, then the time will come when mankind will curse the name of Los Alamos and Hiroshima," he said somberly. "The people of this world must unite, or they will perish."

❊ 15 ❊

In the aftermath of the 2016 election, my wife and I felt lonelier than ever. We'd learned we couldn't change our country, so instead we retreated into it: bought tickets to New Mexico, searched for the deepest deserts we could find. Figuring there must be some place in the world still immune to the world soon to come, we sought refuge where we could: on a mountaintop, on a scenic drive, over margaritas in the hotel bar. "To us," we said, clinking our salt-rimmed glasses. We were just a couple of fragile humans—nothing more. But that afternoon in the hotel bar we pretended to be the braver version of us, the better version of us, the us that believed we could beat back loneliness simply by being together.

✳ **16** ✳

It's the division that spurs the trouble. When an atomic nucleus is split, it releases a neutron, which collides with the radioactive material, which in turn knocks a few more neutrons free. These neutrons begin the chain reaction, the result of which is devastating. Imagine a bottle rocket exploding into a pile of bottle rockets exploding into a warehouse full of bottle rockets. Then, forget all about bottle rockets. A bottle rocket is not a bomb.

✳ **17** ✳

It's easy to feel lonely on a mountaintop. Easy to be alone there, too. In the summer of 1921, after a bout of colitis, Oppenheimer, then 17, convalesced in the wilderness of New Mexico, mounting his horse and taking long rides into the mountains, his pockets filled with chocolate bars.

✳ **18** ✳

Nearly a century later, my wife and I huff 8,000 feet up a mountain. Atop it, we find no liver-eating eagle, no Zeus, only ashes in a wooden box—the remains of somebody's dog. I try to imagine the dog and owner's many treks up this mountain, including the last one. But it's hard. By which I mean I don't want to.

✳ **19** ✳

In the 1930s—when the bomb was still a dream—Oppenheimer, his brother, Frank, and other scientists and students regularly unwound in New Mexico's Pecos wilderness. Provisions were few (whiskey, graham crackers, oats), but the men didn't mind. They just enjoyed their togetherness. Some weeks the men were given maps and horses and told to begin a three-day ride over the mountains. "I'd never been on a horse in my life," one student remarked. But on Oppenheimer's orders, he rode.

✳ **20** ✳

On Oppenheimer's orders they could do anything: enrich, design, even detonate. He and his team didn't just build a bomb, they built a bomb that worked. In the moments following the blast at the Trinity Site, an engineer named Leo Jercinovic crawled on his knees and wondered what he'd just witnessed. A nearby GI answered the question for him: "Buddy," he said, "you just saw the end of the war."

✳ **21** ✳

Back at base camp, physicist George Kistiakowsky saw it differently. Not the end of a war, but the end of the world, instead. "In the last millisecond of the earth's existence," he told an observer, "Man will see what we have just seen."

❋ **22** ❋

"Everything my brother did was special," Frank Oppenheimer recalled. "If he went off into the woods to take a leak he'd come back with a flower. And not to disguise the fact that he'd taken a leak, but to make it an occasion, I guess."

✸ 23 ✸

Days when it rained in the Pecos, Oppenheimer and his cavalry rode through the night, instead. "Imagine this," a former student recalled: "You're riding on a mountain ridge at midnight in the middle of a thunderstorm—lightning hitting all around you—and you come to a fork in the road in the trail. And Robert says, 'This way it's only seven miles home. This way is a little longer but it's much more beautiful.'"

✳ **24** ✳

Oppenheimer always chose the more beautiful path. "Science is not everything," he once remarked, "but science is very beautiful."

❋ 25 ❋

During an early morning drive to Bandelier National Monument, my wife and I find traces of the bomb everywhere we look. We're heading northwest from Santa Fe, passing through the craggy landscape that surrounds us. As we head into the city of Los Alamos, we're greeted by barbwire and caution signs. We are not to turn there or there or there. We are not to enter anywhere without the proper clearance. The longer we drive, the more I realize that the laboratory is not a building but a city unto itself. A city within a city. I can only imagine the interior one, the one beyond my clearance. *How much beauty has been created there*, I marvel as we drive past. *And how much terror, too.*

✸ **26** ✸

On viewing the blast in the Jornada del Muerto desert, Major General Thomas Farrell observed that the golden, purple, blue-gray light lit the mountains "with a clarity and beauty that cannot be described but must be seen to be imagined."

✳ **27** ✳

Roughly translated, Jornada del Muerto means "Journey of the Dead Man."

✳ **28** ✳

Two months after the Trinity Test, a group of men huddled in the desert to examine their destruction up close. They gathered around the remains of the shot tower from which the bomb was dropped. In a photo documenting the event, all the men wear blindingly white overshoes to protect themselves from tracking fallout. And there in the center of the frame is the proud father himself—his left foot on the raised ground like a boxer post-knockout. His fedora sits neatly atop his head as he casts his eyes toward the ground. The men to his left appear funereal, solemn-faced with hands clasped behind their backs. But the men to his right look quite different—dumbfounded, perhaps, or wholly uncertain of what they have created and destroyed.

☀ **29** ☀

In the photo I unearth at the antique store, there's no uncertainty. These are men and women who know how to smile for a camera. Men and women who, after a long day of work, have gathered together to break not nuclei, but bread. My eyes fall to the man I think is Oppenheimer. His expression says precisely what he reported feeling in the moments following the desert blast, a line pulled straight from the *Bhagavad Gita*: "Now, I am become Death, the destroyer of worlds." Either that, or his expression says, *Please pass the potatoes.*

✳ **30** ✳

Having studied Oppenheimer's face during the Trinity Test, General Farrell reported later that in the seconds prior to detonation, Oppenheimer "stared directly ahead." Then, following the "burst of light" and the "growling roar of the explosion," his face "relaxed into an expression of tremendous relief."

※ **31** ※

Some sources report that Oppenheimer stared "directly" ahead. Others report that he stared "dreamily."

✳ 32 ✳

What does one dream of when one has overseen the creation of a nightmare? In a 1960 visit to Japan, 56-year-old Oppenheimer was asked if he regretted his role in the bomb's creation. "I do not regret," he said, "that I had something to do with the technical success of the atomic bomb." Five years later, when interviewed for the CBS Evening News, his answer was more reflective: "When you play a meaningful part in bringing about the death of over 100,000 people and the injury of a comparable number, you naturally don't think of that as—with ease."

✳ **33** ✳

"Why should we always think of what the scientist does," asked scholar George N. Shuster, "and never what he is?"

✳ **34** ✳

Our last night in Santa Fe, I stay awake late and marvel at the photo of the dinner at Los Alamos. After careful study, all I know for certain is that the man I take for Oppenheimer appears to stare dreamily from his place at the head of the table. In the bed to my right, my wife fidgets in her sleep. Finally, I give up trying to read the face under the hotel desk lamp's dim light. I turn off the light, slip into bed, and will both of our bodies to rest.

✹ 35 ✹

For Oppenheimer, detaching was easier than dreaming, and for good reason; he'd been doing it for most of his life. Prior to 1936, he had kept completely disconnected with modern America. He remarked: "I never read a newspaper or a current magazine like *Time* or *Harper's*; I had no radio, no telephone, I learned of the stock market crash in the fall of 1929 only long after the event; the first time I ever voted was in the Presidential election of 1936. To any of my friends, my indifference to contemporary affairs seemed bizarre, and they often chided me with being too much of a highbrow. I was interested in man and his experience; I was deeply interested in my science; but I had no understanding of the relations of man to his society."

❋ 36 ❋

What Oppenheimer wanted most was a place well isolated, a landscape where few people would go. And so, in 1942, Oppenheimer and General Groves got in a car to find the perfect place to build their bomb. When their first location proved less than ideal, they continued on to the next. Oppenheimer knew of a place within an hour's drive of Santa Fe, and Groves agreed to have a look. "As we approached Los Alamos, we came upon a boys' boarding school that occupied part of the area," Groves later wrote. "It was quite evident that this would be an isolated site, with plenty of room for expansion." Oppenheimer breathed a sigh of relief upon the site's selection. He'd done it. He'd found a way to side-step society a while longer.

❄ **37** ❄

By April 1943, as the first wave of scientists descended upon
Los Alamos, they united in their discontent about their living
conditions. "I was rather shocked," noted physicist Hans Bethe.
"I was shocked by the isolation, and I was shocked by the shoddy
buildings." He remarked, too, on the beauty of the snow-covered
mountains in the distance. "But clearly," he said, "we were very
far from anything, very far from anybody."

✳ **38** ✳

Which was, of course, by design. General Groves knew that
isolation meant security; with fewer people around, there was
less risk of a breach. Despite their out-of-the-way location,
Groves's security measures were complicated further due to
the "reluctance of a few of the scientists to recognize the need
for putting some limitations on their personal freedom." He
continued: "For the first year and a half, travel away from
the immediate vicinity of the site was forbidden, except on
laboratory business or in case of emergency. Personal contact
with acquaintances outside the project was discouraged. In the
main these restrictions were accepted as concessions to the
general policy of isolation." Privacy was unpatriotic; loneliness,
a virtue.

✴ **39** ✴

As my wife and I return from our hike at Bandelier, we're stopped at a checkpoint on the edges of Los Alamos. "Driver's license," the guard demands, so I dig it out and hand it over. He eyes my photo, then searches my face for clues. Am I a threat to national security? I wonder. Has my clearance as a citizen been revoked? I hold my breath as his eyes flutter toward my wife, then back toward me. He asks, "Can you vouch for your passenger, sir?" "She's my wife," I say, "of course I can vouch for her." He scowls. Then—seemingly against his better judgment—he lifts the gate and allows us entrance into our country.

✳ **40** ✳

Oppenheimer took easily to the isolated landscape. But in his new role as lab director, there were no more midnight horseback rides through the mountains, no more vanishing acts for days on end. In July 1943, General Groves informed Oppenheimer that his significance to the project demanded safeguards be put in place. He was informed not to ride in any airplanes ("the time saved is not worth the risk"). He was informed, too, to refrain from driving any significant distance ("without suitable protection on any lonely road"). Finally, he was told that even when driving about town ("particularly during hours of darkness"), a guard would need to be dispatched for his protection. "I realize," Groves concluded his letter, "that these precautions may be personally burdensome."

✳ **41** ✳

Years after their relationship ended, Oppenheimer still paid
a price for his association with Jean Tatlock, whose left-wing
activities prompted some to question the scientist's own
patriotism. Oppenheimer had been trying to detach from Tatlock
for years, but it had proven difficult. In June 1943, years after
marrying a German-born biologist named Katherine "Kitty"
Vissering, Oppenheimer agreed to meet Tatlock for a meal in
the midst of a business trip in Berkeley. That night, he slept at
her apartment. We know due to a report filed by the US Army
surveillance team stationed outside Tatlock's home.

❊ **43** ❊

To do what he did—to build what he built—it was imperative that Oppenheimer detach. Professor James Hijiya writes: "When he thought about the bomb—his duty to build it, other men's duty to decide how to use it, and his detachment from the fruits of his work—he believed that he had done the right thing. It was not that Oppenheimer had no misgivings about what he did at Los Alamos. It was just that his philosophy enabled him to overcome it."

✸ **43** ✸

His philosophy proved enabling. For two years, he woke each morning, rose from his bed, and did his best to build a bomb. "If you are a scientist, you believe that it is good to find out how the world works," Oppenheimer told Los Alamos workers in November 1945. "When you see something that is technically sweet, you go ahead and do it and you argue about what to do about it only after you have had your technical success."

✳ **44** ✳

But following his technical success, the argument over the bomb's usage was moot. Scientist Leo Szilard and 68 colleagues petitioned President Harry S. Truman to "make greater efforts to avoid having to drop the bomb on the Japanese populace." The president heard a different message: that he now possessed the means to end a war. And perhaps, if he was lucky, all wars.

※ **45** ※

Fearing nuclear attack, in 1951 the Federal Civil Defense Administration created a nine-minute film starring Bert the Turtle, a cartoon terrapin wearing a bow tie and helmet. As his theme song notes, Bert never got hurt because "he knew just what to do." When a monkey hangs from a cartoon tree, dangling a firecracker, Bert retreats into the safety of his shell. The firecracker crackles, but Bert remains unscathed.

❊ **46** ❊

A generation of school-aged children swallowed the lie that
we fed them. Their parents swallowed it, too. Not because
they believed it, but because hope was more palatable than
hopelessness. The truth, of course, was that no "duck and
cover" technique could ever deflect a bomb. If those school-aged
children had found themselves within the blast zone, they would
have died there: crouched beneath their desks, ducked and
covered, humming that turtle's song.

✳ **47** ✳

By detaching, Oppenheimer found a way to live a normal life. Found a way to pack his pipe with tobacco without thinking the word *detonate*. Found a way to enjoy a poem, or a film, or to water the plants without considering radiation. Everything was always fine as long as he detached. Decades later, my wife and I try the opposite approach. We turn in toward each other to avoid turning out toward the new world. We lift our glasses in a hotel bar. "To us," we say, and we mean it.

✳ **48** ✳

What's a man like Oppenheimer do once his wife and two children fall asleep? Does he retreat to his study, dim the lights, and watch the blast replay on his reel-to-reel? Does he stare directly (or dreamily) into that expanding cloud and wonder what he's done? Maybe he just draws the shades, walks the trash to the curb, brushes his teeth, and calls it a night.

☀ **49** ☀

What do I do when my wife and two children fall asleep? Lately, I retreat to my study, dim the lights, and watch footage from Oppenheimer's blasts.

✳ 50 ✳

Nearly a decade after the Trinity Test, Oppenheimer's loneliness grew. Following a public hearing in 1954, he was stripped of his security clearance. "He retreated," explained a friend. "And returned to a simpler way of life." The Oppenheimer family took refuge on a few acres in the Virgin Islands. There, Oppenheimer boarded his sailboat and allowed the wind to take him where it would. Who's to say what he saw out in that water, or if he saw anything at all. Maybe seeing nothing was precisely what he hoped to see most.

✳ **51** ✳

In the 1954 US Atomic Energy Commission security hearings, Isidor Rabi—the physicist who, a decade prior, had guessed destruction best—spoke in Oppenheimer's defense. He cited the man's many contributions—innovations in physics, nuclear policy, the creation of the blasted bomb itself. His defense failed to rouse the committee members, prompting an exasperated Rabi to remark, "What more do you want? Mermaids?"

✳ **52** ✳

On January 4, 1944, Jean Tatlock got away from the world for good. In her suicide note, she mentioned feeling "disgusted with everything" and "paralyzed somehow." She did not say she suffered from a broken heart, though she might've. The letter continued: "To those who loved me and helped me, all love and courage." If Tatlock felt lonely, she needn't have. Even at the time of her death, she was being surveilled.

✳ **53** ✳

On my last day in New Mexico, I bring the antique-store photo to the National Atomic Testing Museum in Albuquerque. I pull the archivist aside, show her the photo, say, "It's him, isn't it?" The archivist takes one look and assures me it is not. I'm dumbstruck. *How could it not be?* I wonder. *How could the story I've built for the man not be the story that's true?*

❊ **54** ❊

Of the many things we do not know, here's one thing we do: stories, like bombs, are difficult to reconstruct in the aftermath. As are our relationships. As is the world itself. And in the end— once our world or some part of it unravels—all we have left is the aftermath. The time before we'll just call prologue. The good ol' days. The moment when we never felt alone.

❋ **55** ❋

At dawn in Albuquerque, a sheet of ice glosses the roads. My wife and I grip the armrests tight as the shuttle bus spins and spins. We are less than a mile from the airport, and we both know we're better off walking. So we do, our wheeled suitcases leaving dual tracks in the snow. Already we have hiked mountains together, enjoyed scenic drives together, vouched for one another, and sipped margaritas in a hotel bar. What, after all of this, is a short little walk in the snow? As we head toward the terminal, I say, "Well, an imperfect end to our otherwise perfect trip." She smiles. I smile. We mean it.

✳ 56 ✳

Following the Trinity Test, Oppenheimer was said to have taken a walk alone in the desert. Along the way he came upon a turtle lying shell-down in the sand. The shock wave from the blast had caused that turtle's predicament, but since he was alone, there was nothing to be done about it. No one there to right the wrong. Enter Oppenheimer, who crouched alongside the creature, studying its helplessness with eyes as blue as mountain flowers. Then, ever so slowly, he extended a hand, reached for the shell, and returned that turtle to his feet.

☀ **57** ☀

How easy it is, sometimes, to set right our wrongs. Yet at other times, how impossible.

WORKS CITED

Bird, Kai, and Martin J. Sherwin. *American Prometheus: The Triumph and Tragedy of J. Robert Oppenheimer.* New York: A. A. Knopf, 2005.

Cassidy, David C. *J. Robert Oppenheimer and the American Century.* New York: Pi Press, 2005.

Cathcart, Brian. "Atomised." *New Statesman.* Jan. 10, 2008.

The Day after Trinity: J. Robert Oppenheimer and the Bomb. Dir. John H. Else. Pyramid Films, 1981. DVD.

Federal Civil Defense Administration. "Duck and Cover." 1951. Nuclear Vault. Youtube.com.

Groves, Leslie. *Now It Can Be Told: The Story of the Manhattan Project.* New York: Harper & Row, 1962.

Hijiya, James A. "The Gita of J. Robert Oppenheimer." *Proceedings of the American Philosophical Society* 144.2 (June 2000).

Jungk, Robert. *Brighter than a Thousand Suns: A Personal History of the Atomic Scientists.* New York: Harcourt, Brace, 1958.

Lamont, Lansing. *Day of Trinity.* New York: Atheneum, 1965.

Laurence, William. *Dawn Over Zero: The Story of the Atomic Bomb.* New York: Alfred A. Knopf, 1946.

——. *Men and Atoms: The Discovery, the Uses and the Future of Atomic Energy.* New York: Simon and Schuster, 1959.

"Oppenheimer's Travel Guidance." *Atomic Archive.* National Science Digital Library. 2015.

Oz, Mehmet. "The New Loneliness." *Huffington Post.* Sept. 12, 2016.

Pais, Abraham, and Robert P. Crease. *J. Robert Oppenheimer: A Life.* Oxford: Oxford University Press, 2006.

Rhodes, Richard. *The Making of the Atomic Bomb.* New York: Simon and Schuster, 1986.

"The Trinity Test." *The Manhattan Project: An Interactive History*. osti.gov/opennet/manhattan-project-history/Events/1945/trinity.htm.

Wellerstein, Alex. "The First Light of Trinity." *New Yorker*. July 16, 2015.

FRAGMENTS FOR MEDGAR

I've been driving through Dixie for days when at last I enter Jackson, Mississippi, a disconcertingly quiet place. It is a contrast to the smaller southern towns I've recently visited, many of whose black citizens seemed curious—and maybe a little uneasy—about the white guy in the rental car asking questions about civil rights.

"I'm here to gather stories for a book project on the civil-rights era," I explained. But as with all projects—and road trips—my work had taken an unexpected turn.

Just a few days in, I discovered that many of the people who'd lived those stories I was after were no longer alive. I didn't know how to persuade the dead to talk, nor did I understand my role in trying to tell the stories I did find. All I knew was that the world was losing people—and stories—at an alarming rate. Desperate to capture what I could, I drove to Jackson. Foot on the accelerator, ear cocked toward the wind, I prepared myself to listen.

*

Around 1933, eight-year-old Medgar Evers watched Willie Tingle get dragged through the streets of their town, Decatur, Mississippi—70 miles west of Jackson. Tingle, a family friend, allegedly had made the mistake of talking back to a white woman. He was dragged, shot, and hung from a tree. Medgar and his brother Charles passed Tingle's blood-stained clothes daily while walking to school. For black boys in Mississippi the message was clear: This is what happens if you don't keep your eyes low and your feet moving.

*

Twenty-two years later, a 14-year-old boy named Emmett Till was also alleged to have talked back to a white woman. One night soon after, in August 1955, he was abducted by Roy Bryant and J. W. Milam in Money, Mississippi. They beat him, shot him, tied a gin fan round his neck, then dumped him into the Tallahatchie River. Shortly after his body was recovered, Emmett Till's mother made a choice, one that ensured that white America could no longer avert its eyes from racial violence. Leaving his casket open, weeping as she stared at the face that no longer resembled her son, Mamie Till forced us to look. Photographer David Jackson snapped a photo of Emmett's bludgeoned body, published it in the September 1955 issue of *Jet* magazine, and extended the horror to every American who dared flip through its pages.

"I wanted the world to see what they did to my baby," Mamie Till remarked. The world looked. Sometimes we still look. That is, when we're not averting our eyes.

*

Decades after Medgar Evers passed Willie Tingle's bloodstained clothes, he was dispatched to investigate the murder of Emmett Till. Evers talked, he listened, he tried to secure all the witness testimony he could. His efforts went unrewarded. The all-white jury for the Till case deliberated for 67 minutes.

"If we hadn't stopped to drink pop," one juror remarked, "it wouldn't have taken that long."

*

"The exhibition of the brutalized black body," writes

southern literature scholar Minrose Gwin, "is mired in a complex history of white voyeurism."

*

I am aware of being the white voyeur in this scenario as I approach Medgar Evers's home in Jackson. Today it's formally called the Medgar Evers Home Museum, though it holds no regular hours. In the weeks preceding my visit, I'd placed a call to Minnie Watson, an archivist at nearby Tougaloo College, who agreed to give me the tour. But upon pulling the car to the side of the road just outside the house, I am the only one there: the voyeur, the tragedy tourist. The white man in the predominantly black neighborhood—much like Evers's killer. I've been worried about this feeling since the moment I returned to the South. Worried, too, by the baggage I bring with my white body. The South is my former home, but it never quite felt like home when I lived there. Instead, it felt like a place I was inhabiting for four years of graduate school. More than a few born-and-raised southerners were quick to peg me for what I was: some dumb-cluck northern carpetbagger who didn't know the first thing about football, barbecue, or history.

*

Before Medgar Evers was murdered, he was a father, a husband, and an NAACP field secretary. Raised in Mississippi, he knew its backroads and its fishing holes and the kind of foliage-filled lots that might hide an assassin. Shortly after breakfast on the day he was killed, he peered out at the thicket of shrubs in the lot across the street. He studied it curiously, then slipped inside his blue Oldsmobile and drove away.

*

Myrlie Beasley was a freshman at Mississippi's Alcorn State University when she first met Medgar Evers, the junior class president and football star who'd taken an interest in her.

"Although for a week I thought his name was Edgar Evans," she wrote in her memoir, *For Us, the Living*. He often walked her back to her dorm following choir practice or frequented the music studio where she played piano. Some days they'd drive to the Civil War battlefield in nearby Vicksburg, two lovestruck college kids strolling among the cannons.

*

A few hours before parking in front of Evers's home, I visit civil-rights activist Hezekiah Watkins. Over coffee he tells me about the time he was jailed with Dr. King, and of his years working alongside James Bevel. He tells me, too, how on the evening of June 11, 1963, he was handed a .22 caliber pistol and told to keep an eye on the perimeter surrounding the church where Evers was scheduled to speak.

"I was about 16," Watkins says. "Was I going to use it? I didn't know. But I had it. It was in my pocket while I was riding my bicycle."

*

It wasn't until Medgar Evers's involvement in the Emmett Till case that Myrlie Evers began to fear for her husband's life.

"Medgar would leave the house for one of his trips to the Delta, and I could feel my stomach contract in cold fear that I would never see him again," she later wrote. Night after night, to her great relief, he returned home from the Delta.

*

One evening Myrlie Evers answered the phone to hear a slew of insults. She could only endure it for so long. After she hollered, "Why don't you go to hell?," her husband got on the line and talked to the caller. The call lasted for some time, and ended, Myrlie recalled, with her husband and the caller speaking "almost cordially." Upon hanging up, Medgar turned to his wife. "Myrlie," he said, "don't ever do what you did. If you can't take it, just put the phone down. But don't curse at them. You can sometimes win them over if you are just patient enough."

*

But how often have we known a bullet to be patient? Or a noose, or a knife, or a flame? I'll never know the weight of a gin fan—merely the weight of a white man writing about a black body tied to one. A weight that seems hardly worth mentioning at all.

*

A few days before I visit Medgar Evers's home, an interviewee thanks me for gathering these civil-rights stories.

I tell him it's nothing.

"It's not nothing," he says. "And it's important that it's coming from a guy like you, from a white man." A smile escapes as he prepares for his punchline: "It's proof that y'all ain't bad."

*

On June 7, 1963—less than a week before Evers's murder—an FBI report noted his concern that his phones were being bugged.

"Evers' suspicions that his office and home phones are being tapped date back to three or four years ago," the report reads. "These suspicions were aroused because of unusual amount of static on telephone lines and a feeling as if he were listening in a vacuum."

In a memo dated the following day, the FBI director was informed that the Southern Bell Telephone and Telegraph Co. of Jackson had checked the phone lines at Medgar's office and home and found nothing to indicate a tap.

*

In late May 1963, a firebomb was hurled into the Evers's carport. It was after midnight, the kids were asleep, and Myrlie woke with a start. She ran outside, reached for the garden hose,

and doused the remaining flames. Later that night she and her
husband wandered their home, taking stock of all they hadn't
lost.

"I don't know what I'd do if anything ever happened to
you or the children because of what I'm doing," Medgar confided.

"It's not us," Myrlie replied. "It's you they're after."

*

The following morning, upon hearing of the bombing,
nine-year-old Darrell Evers announced to his family that he
hated white people.

"Then you're wrong," Medgar said. "You're hurting
yourself. You shouldn't hate white people. You shouldn't hate
anyone. That's no way to live." He glanced toward his son,
softening: "It's not good for a little boy's heart to hate."

*

Lying in bed beside Myrlie one night, Medgar said, "If I
go tonight, if I go next week, if I go next year, I feel I'm ready to
go." He had plenty of reasons to believe his life was in danger:
the marches, the mass meetings, the voter registration drives.
But most of all, his refusal to keep his head down and his feet
moving. Shortly after becoming Mississippi's NAACP field
secretary, he was one of nine people placed on a so-called death
list, and in the days leading up to his murder, he was warned of
renewed threats against his life. One day in June 1963, Myrlie
ironed a week's worth of her husband's shirts. Medgar thanked
her, but offered, too, that he wasn't going to need that many.

*

Long before their house was firebombed, Evers gathered
his three children and asked, "What is the safest place in the
house?" The children wandered their home, eyeing the kitchen,
the living room, the bedrooms. Eventually, much to their father's
satisfaction, they agreed that the bathroom was likely the safest

place. No one picked the driveway. Even the children knew better than that.

*

Father's Day was just a few days away, and in anticipation, eight-year-old Reena had already completed her handmade card. She'd pressed wildflowers in its interior, and with her red crayon scrawled, "I love you, Daddy."

*

At a few minutes past midnight on June 12, 1963, the Evers children heard their father's Oldsmobile rumble into the drive.

"Daddy's home!" Reena called. They leapt up, preparing to meet him.

*

Outside, hiding amid the honeysuckle in the lot across the street, a fertilizer salesman from Greenwood, Mississippi, watched Evers step out from his car.

*

The bullet bored through Medgar Evers's right shoulder before hurtling through the living room window. It hit a wall, then ricocheted off the fridge before coming to a halt on the kitchen counter, where it lay, suddenly docile and dumb. Like a crumb to be wiped away.

*

Reena did exactly as she'd been trained: she hit the floor alongside her brothers. Together, the Evers children crawled to the bathroom, the safest place, and waited for the danger to pass.

*

Myrlie Evers flipped on the carport light to find her husband facedown in the drive. In his outstretched hand was the key to their home. Piled alongside him were the shirts he'd retrieved from the car. Emblazoned across their front was a slogan he had been advocating for years: "Jim Crow Must Go."

*

The children heard their mother scream and pulled themselves from the bathtub. They crowded around their father, pleaded with him to get up. Across the street, a fertilizer salesmen removed himself from the honeysuckle. He dropped his rifle into some nearby bushes, then drove away from the scene. Meanwhile, others rushed toward it: friends, neighbors, anyone who thought they might help. A few men removed Reena's mattress from her bed to use as a gurney for her father. He and the mattress were placed in the back of a car, and the children watched as their father disappeared.

"Mommy, don't cry," Reena soothed. "Maybe Daddy can get some rest now."

*

Medgar Evers was driven to a local hospital where, after some debate, the doctors agreed to admit the black man. He died within an hour. His final words: "Turn me loose."

*

Minnie Watson, a tall, middle-aged black woman with salt-and-pepper hair, arrives at the Medgar Evers Home Museum shortly after I do. I thank her for her time.

"No problem," she says as she flips through her keys. "Just give me a moment to set up."

I loiter in the front yard as she enters the house, opening the curtains, flicking on the lights.

"Okay," she says, "come on in."

I enter through the side door and stand in the living room. She tells me to make myself at home.

*

This is not my home. Those are not my beige couches. And that upright piano, that is not mine, either. Those are not my children in the photos. Those are not my children's mattresses on the floor. Those are not their toys, not their books, not their stuffed animals propped against the pillows. Those are not my clothes in the closet. That is not my change on the dresser. Not my cufflinks, not my pocketknife, not my mirror. Yet when I look into that mirror, that is certainly me reflected back—a white man from the North, in a house not his own. What am I to make of my expression? Is it sorrow or complicity?

*

In a 1958 issue of *Ebony* magazine, fresh-faced, burgeoning civil-rights leader Medgar Evers acknowledged his willingness to die for the cause.

"And as long as God gives me strength to work and try to make things real for my children, I'm going to work for it—," he said, "even if it means making the ultimate sacrifice."

*

Forty-five years after Medgar Evers's death, I discover a letter in an Alabama archive. It's addressed to University of Alabama president O. C. Carmichael, under whose purview desegregation was first attempted in 1956. The letter writer informed Carmichael that segregation must be preserved "at all costs." Seven years later, on the very day the University of Alabama successfully desegregated, the letter writer—a fertilizer salesman named Byron De La Beckwith—positioned himself in the honeysuckle across the street from Medgar Evers's home. He lifted his eye to the scope, his finger to the trigger, and tried to preserve segregation at all costs.

*

Over a cup of gumbo at the Mayflower Café, award-winning *Clarion-Ledger* reporter Jerry Mitchell tells me how he gets murderers to talk. The trick, Mitchell says, smoothing his tie, is to go to them. In April 1990, Mitchell made the long drive from Jackson to Signal Mountain, Tennessee, to talk to Byron De

La Beckwith. Mitchell arrived midafternoon and, for the next six hours, listened as Beckwith ranted about his troubles with black people. After filling a notebook, Mitchell thanked Beckwith for speaking with him, then stood to leave.

"It was starting to get dark," Mitchell tells me, "and he insisted on walking me out to the car. I was like, 'Really, that's okay. I think I can handle it.' He walked me out anyway."

The pair stepped outside into the evening, and as Mitchell reached for the door of his car, Beckwith offered a warning: "If you write positive things about white Caucasian Christians, then God will bless you. If you write negative things about white Caucasian Christians, God will punish you. And if God does not punish you," he added, "then several individuals will do it for Him."

*

Minnie Watson walks me to the carport where the hint of a rust-colored bloodstain remains. She points to it, then lifts her finger to direct my eyes to the location across the street where the gun was fired. She tells me that Evers's home has no front door because a front door would've left him and his family exposed to an assassin's bullet. The bedroom windows were built high and the children's mattresses kept low as further protection from bullets.

"Now then," she says, "any questions?"

*

I know how you transform a man into a martyr, but how do you transform a martyr back into a man?

*

A century before Medgar Evers's murder, and 40 miles west of Jackson, the Siege of Vicksburg raged. After a 48-day campaign, the Union emerged victorious, having crippled one of the last vestiges of Confederate power along the Mississippi.

On that ground, nearly 8,000 soldiers were killed and another 30,000 captured. In the 1958 photograph featured in *Ebony*, the Evers family stands with their backs to the camera. Myrlie holds her children's hands—Reena on the left, Darrell on the right. To the right of them stands Medgar, his left hand resting softly atop his young son's head.

"The civil war battlefield at Vicksburg should remind all of us of the futility of armed conflict," Medgar informed the journalist. "Despite its history, it is one of the state's most beautiful spots."

*

"Medgar, of all people, was not blind to Mississippi's flaws, but he seemed convinced they could be corrected," Myrlie wrote. "He loved his state with hope and only rarely with despair. It was the hope that sustained him. It never left him. Despair came infrequently, and a day of hunting or fishing dispelled it. The love remained."

*

In the summer of 1996, on another hot night in Jackson, it happened all over again. A black man walked toward the side door of Medgar Evers's home. This time, though, when the shot rang out, cameras were rolling. On cue, the actor playing Evers pulled a cord to trigger the blood package strapped to his back. The blood—a mixture of glycerin and chocolate syrup—went everywhere. According to Willie Morris's *The Ghost of Medgar Evers*, this was only the third time in American cinematic history that the movie version of a murder had been filmed at the home where the actual murder took place. How unsettling it must've been for the longtime neighbors, who'd witnessed Medgar's murder all those years before. And how unsettling for Medgar's brother Charles, who chose to bear witness to the scene. Chose to watch as an actor who looked like his brother toppled in his brother's driveway again and again. Watched, too, as the miracle occurred: the man rose from the dead, brushed himself off, and did it all again.

*

Leaving Medgar Evers's home, I wonder why I came at all. Was it the voyeur in me? Or the story seeker?

Or maybe, I think, because not averting my eyes seemed like the least I could do.

*

I spend the rest of the afternoon walking the streets of Jackson. I spot the dome of Russell C. Davis Planetarium and take advantage of the opportunity to vacate our planet for a while. I fork over five bucks, then settle into my seat in the nearly empty auditorium. Tilting my head skyward, I try to pay attention to the narrator's booming voice. But all I can think about is a man named Medgar wandering a battlefield alone. And a boy named Emmett toeing the waterline of a mud-and-blood-filled river. Inside that dark theater, the combination of air-conditioning and the narrator's voice eventually lulls me to sleep. It is a glorious sleep, and I dream myself back home to my family. When I awake some time later, all I see above me are stars. I rub my eyes, regain my bearings, and listen to the booming voice over the loudspeakers. "Let us take comfort in the stability of our own world," the narrator says.

*

"You happy?" the waitress asks.

I'm alone in a booth in a restaurant somewhere in Jackson.

"Hmm?" I ask, trying hard to focus on the question.

"I said," she repeats, slower this time, "are you happy?"

I open my mouth to speak. But the answer—even if I had one—never leaves my throat.

WORKS CITED

Evers, Medgar, and Francis Mitchell. "Why I Live in Mississippi."
    Ebony. 1958.

Evers, Myrlie, and William Peters. *For Us, the Living*. New York:
    Doubleday, 1967.

Evers-Williams, Myrlie, and Manning Marable, eds. *The
    Autobiography of Medgar Evers: A Hero's Life and Legacy
    Revealed Through His Writings, Letters, and Speeches*. New
    York: Basic Civitas, 2006.

Gwin, Minrose. *Remembering Medgar Evers: Writing the Long Civil
    Rights Movement*. Athens: University of Georgia Press,
    2013.

"Medgar Evers." Federal Bureau of Investigation Files. July 15,
    2017. https://vault.fbi.gov/Medgar%20Evers.

Mitchell, Jerry. Interview. May 26, 2016.

———. "Simply 'Daddy': Reena Evers-Everette Shares Memories
    of Medgar." *Clarion-Ledger*. June 1, 2015.

Morris, Willie. *The Ghost of Medgar Evers: A Tale of Race, Murder,
    Mississippi and Hollywood*. New York: Random House,
    1998.

Nossiter, Adam. *Of Long Memory: Mississippi and the Murder of
    Medgar Evers*. New York: Addison-Wesley, 1994.

"O. C. Carmichael Collection." W. S. Hoole Special Collections
    Library. University of Alabama.

Watkins, Hezekiah. Interview. May 28, 2016.

Watson, Minnie. Interview. May 28, 2016.

Whitfield, Stephen. *A Death in the Delta: The Story of Emmett Till*.
    Baltimore: John Hopkins University Press, 1991.

Williams, Michael Vinson. *Medgar Evers: Mississippi Martyr*.
    Fayetteville: University of Arkansas Press, 2013.

ABOUT THE AUTHOR

B. J. Hollars is the author of several books, most recently *The Road South: Personal Stories of the Freedom Riders*; *Flock Together: A Love Affair With Extinct Birds*; and *From the Mouths of Dogs: What Our Pets Teach Us About Life, Death, and Being Human.* An associate professor of English at the University of Wisconsin-Eau Claire, he lives a simple existence with his wife, their children, and their dog.

www.bjhollars.com